Maps, Maps, Maps!

by Kelly Boswell

CAPSTONE PRESS
a capstone imprint

A+ Books are published by Capstone Press,
1710 Roe Crest Drive, North Mankato, Minnesota 56003
www.capstonepub.com

Library of Congress Cataloging-in-Publication Data
Boswell, Kelly.
 Maps, maps, maps! / by Kelly Boswell.
    pages cm. — (A+ books : Displaying information)
 Includes index.
 Summary: "Introduces types of maps and how they are used"—Provided by publisher.
 ISBN 978-1-4765-0262-5 (library binding)
 ISBN 978-1-4765-3339-1 (paperback)
 ISBN 978-1-4765-3343-8 (ebook PDF)
 1. Maps—Juvenile literature. I. Title.
 GA105.6.B66 2014
 912—dc23   2012050515

Editorial Credits
Kristen Mohn, editor; Juliette Peters, designer; Marcie Spence, media researcher;
Charmaine Whitman, production specialist

Photo Credits
Capstone Studio: Karon Dubke, cover (middle), 1, 4 (left), 4–5, 6, 7, 8, 9, 15, 16, 21, 24–25,
32; iStockphoto: BirdsofPrey, 10, CEFutcher, 20, Rubberball, 14; Shutterstock: Alex and
Anna, 18–19, bahri altay, cover (bottom), Debu55y, 12–13, Diana Rich, 4 (right), Haizul, 3, 5,
32, jorgen mcleman, 17, Pedro Nogueira, cover (bottom), Seamartini Graphics, cover (top),
Stawek, 26–27, Teschanko Irina, cover (bottom), Tribalium, 29, wavebreakmedia, 22–23

Note to Parents, Teachers, and Librarians
This Displaying Information book uses full color photographs and a nonfiction format to
introduce the concept of maps. This book is designed to be read aloud to a pre-reader or
to be read independently by an early reader. Photographs help listeners and early readers
understand the text and concepts discussed. The book encourages further learning by
including the following sections: Table of Contents, Glossary, Read More, Internet Sites,
and Index. Early readers may need assistance using these features.

Printed in the United States of America in North Mankato, Minnesota.
032014   008072R

Table of Contents

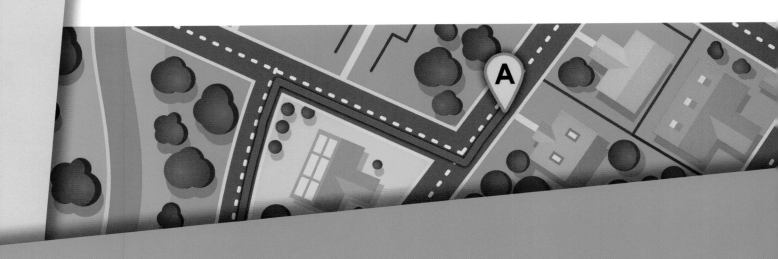

Maps All Around

Look around and you'll see maps. There are maps in parks, shopping malls, and museums. There are maps of your town or city, maps of your country, and maps of the world.

Keep Right at Main Street

1/2 mi

1:30
15.5 mi
ETA 1:45 pm

11:47

MENU

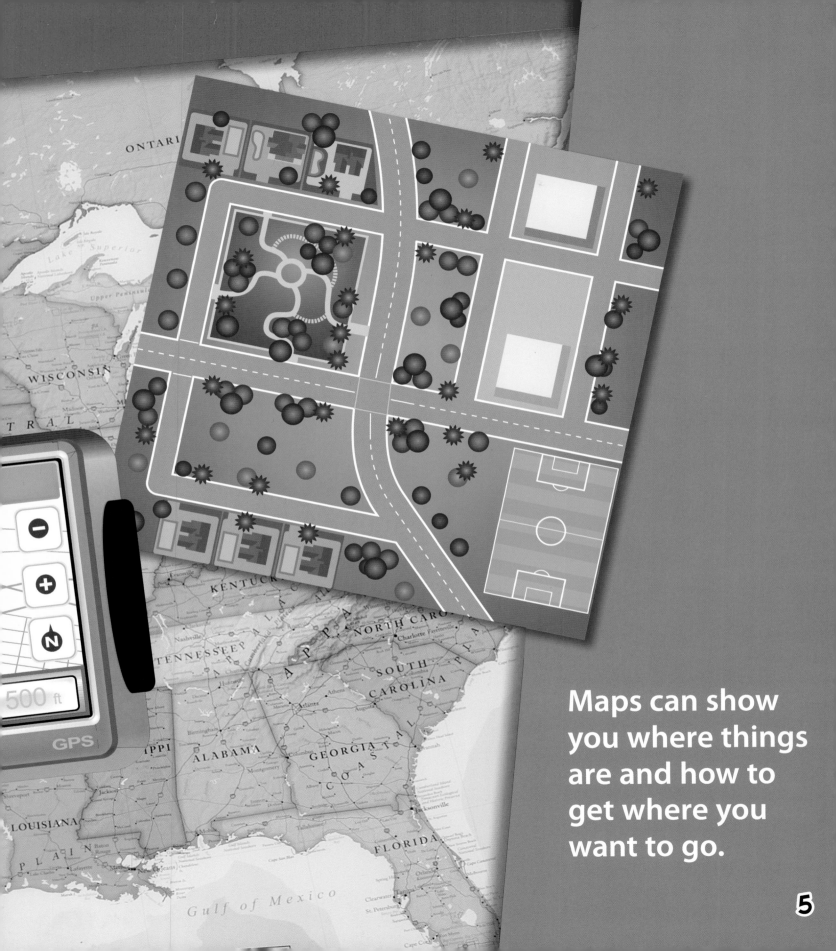

Maps can show
you where things
are and how to
get where you
want to go.

Brady is making a city. He has houses, buildings, roads, a river, and a train track in his city.

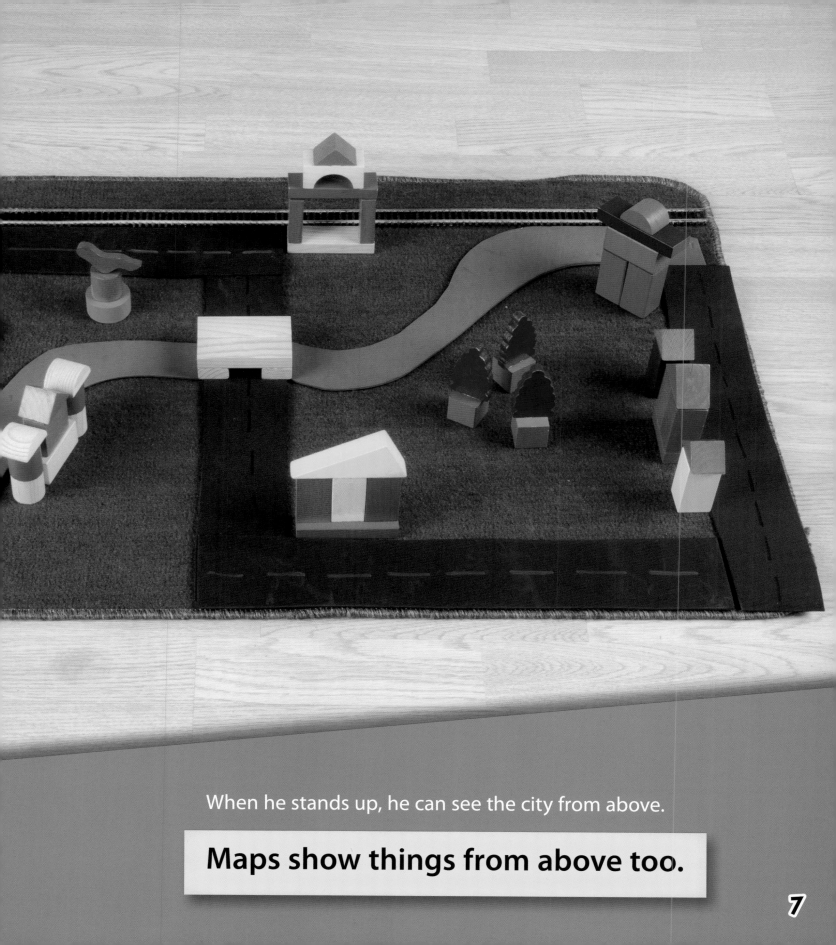

When he stands up, he can see the city from above.

Maps show things from above too.

Brady makes a map to show the parts of his city.

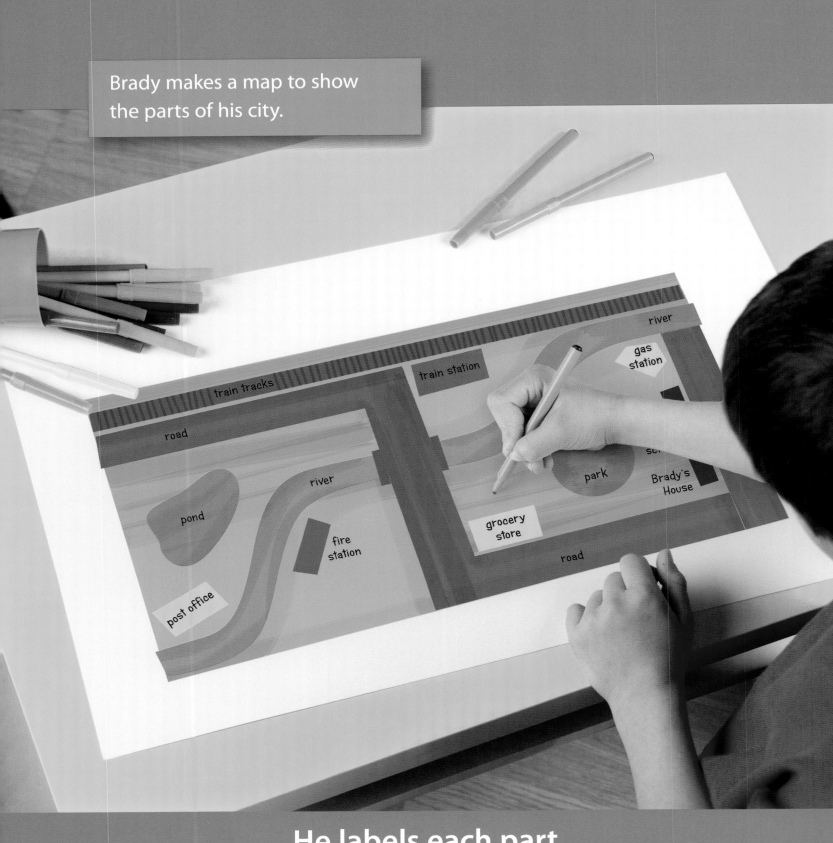

train tracks

road

river

pond

fire
station

post office

train station

gas
station

park

Brady's
House

grocery
store

road

river

He labels each part.

Now he needs a title for the map. The title tells others what the map is showing.

Brady City

train tracks

road

river

pond

Map Symbols

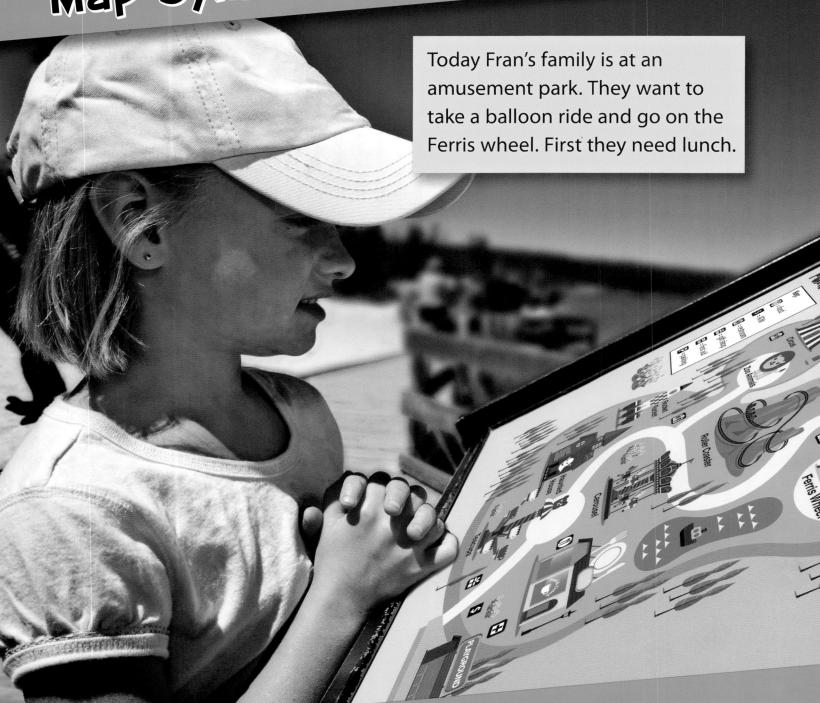

Today Fran's family is at an amusement park. They want to take a balloon ride and go on the Ferris wheel. First they need lunch.

They use a map to find out which way to go.

10

There are symbols at the side or bottom of most maps.

Each symbol stands for something on the map. The box that shows these symbols is called a key or a legend. It explains what the symbols mean.

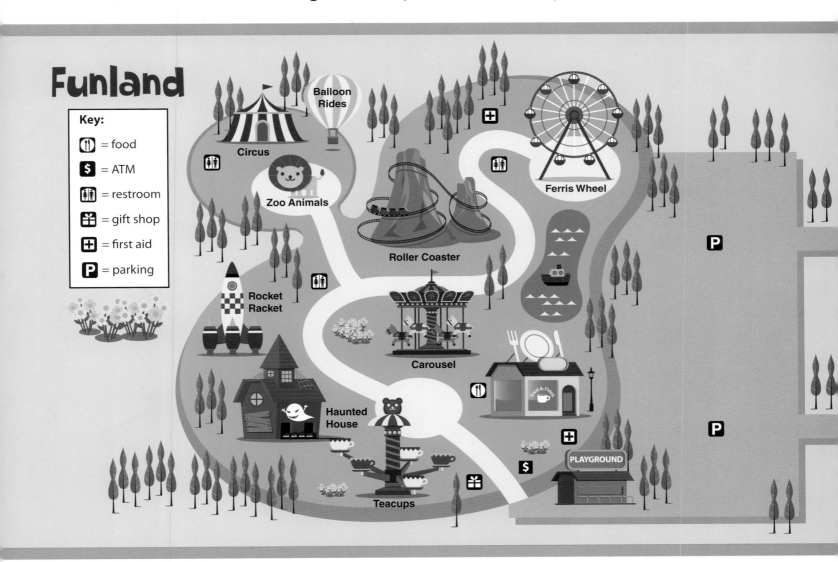

Funland

Key:
- 🍴 = food
- $ = ATM
- 🚻 = restroom
- 🎁 = gift shop
- ✚ = first aid
- P = parking

Balloon Rides

Circus

Zoo Animals

Ferris Wheel

Roller Coaster

Rocket Racket

Carousel

Haunted House

Teacups

Food & Drink

PLAYGROUND

P

Where can they eat lunch?

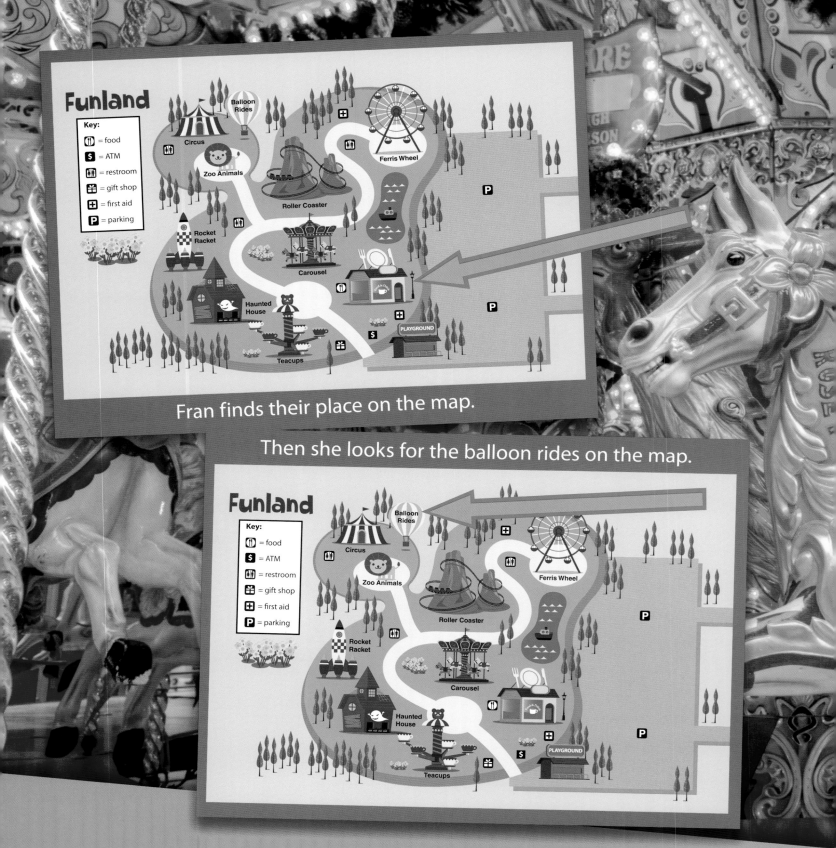

Fran finds their place on the map.

Then she looks for the balloon rides on the map.

They want to get from here to there.

Funland

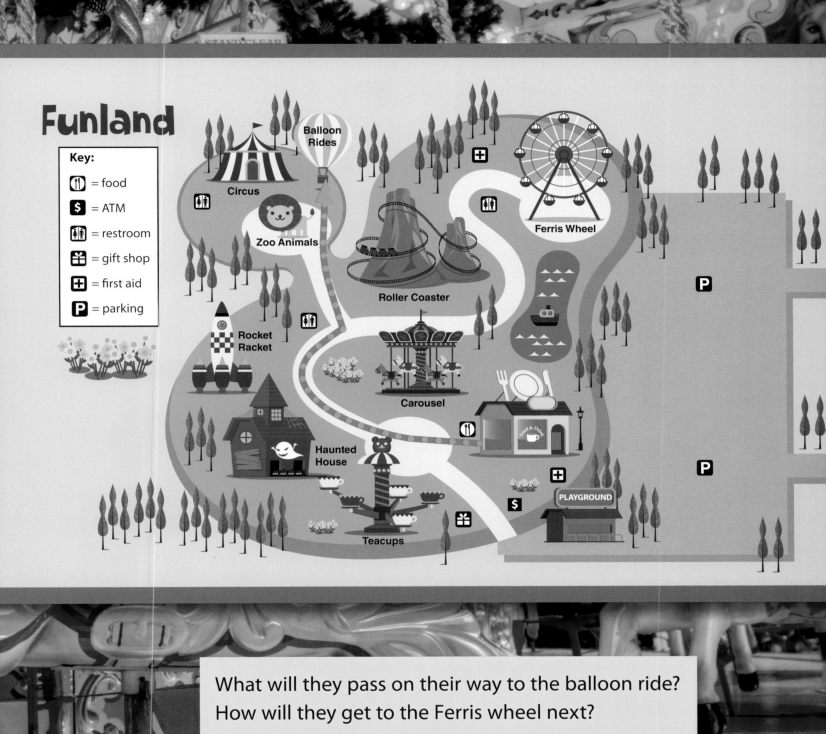

Key:

- 🍴 = food
- 💲 = ATM
- 🚻 = restroom
- 🎁 = gift shop
- ✚ = first aid
- 🅿 = parking

Balloon Rides

Circus

Zoo Animals

Ferris Wheel

Roller Coaster

Rocket Racket

Carousel

Food & Drink

Haunted House

Teacups

PLAYGROUND

What will they pass on their way to the balloon ride?
How will they get to the Ferris wheel next?

Compass Rose

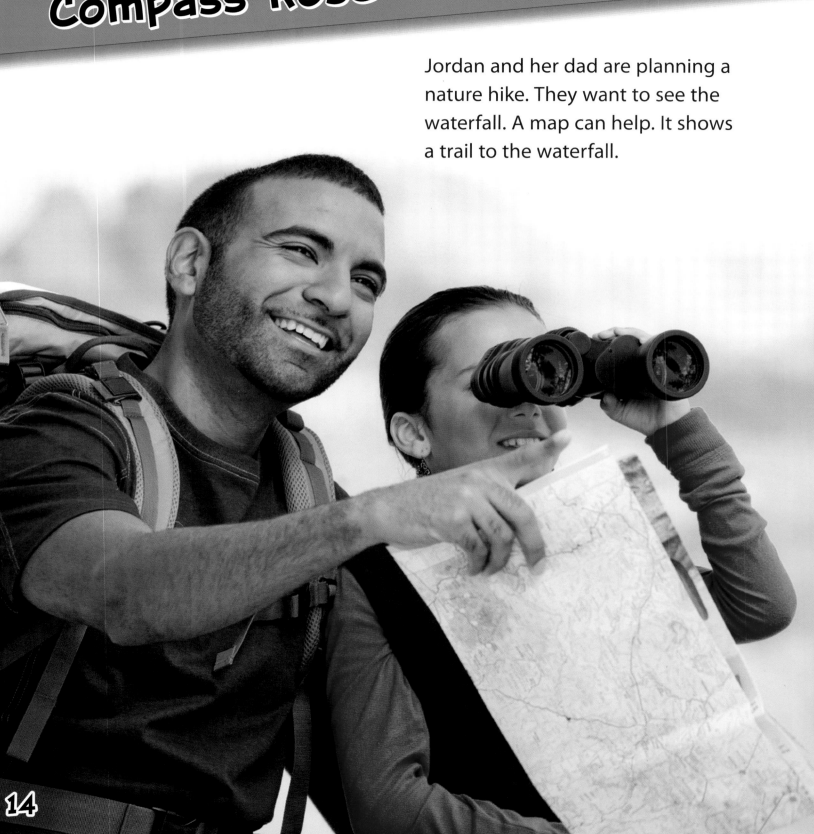

Jordan and her dad are planning a nature hike. They want to see the waterfall. A map can help. It shows a trail to the waterfall.

Eagle Lake Park

Eagle Lake

You Are Here

Key

Mountain Hill

River Bridge Trail

Waterfall Road

N
W E
S

This symbol is called a compass rose. It shows north, south, east, and west on the map. The waterfall is to the west.

Let's go!

Road Maps

Jade has been invited to play at Kayla's house. A computer can help her find the way. Jade's mom types in their home address and Kayla's address.

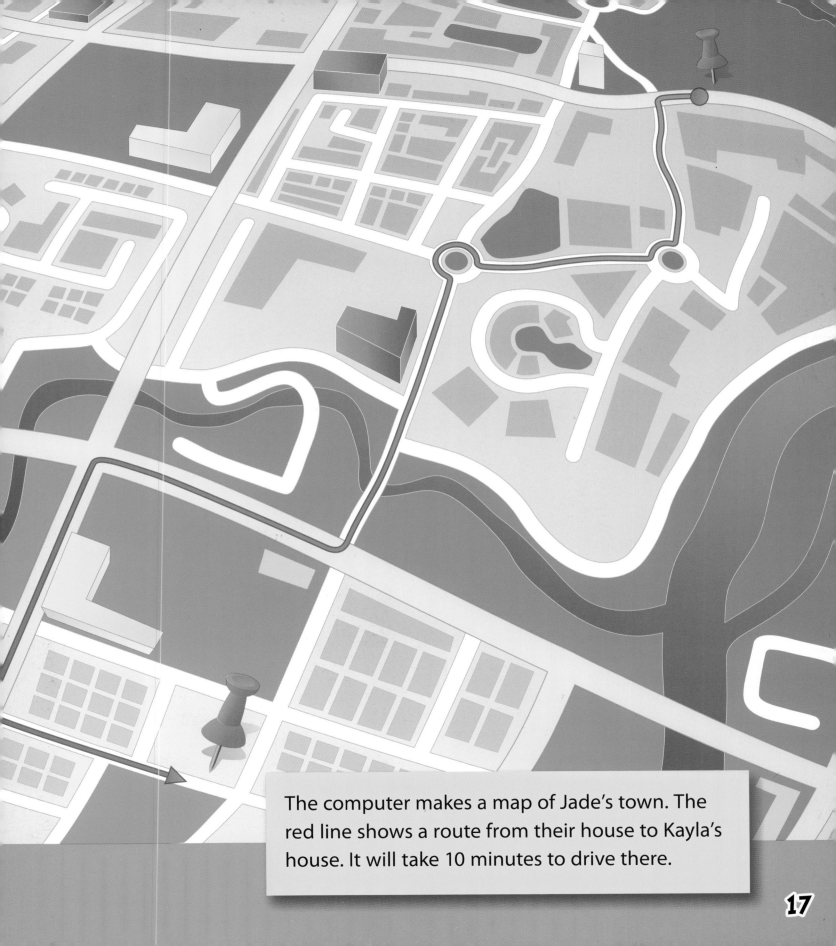

The computer makes a map of Jade's town. The red line shows a route from their house to Kayla's house. It will take 10 minutes to drive there.

Political Maps

Some maps show a whole country.

A political map shows the boundaries between states or countries.

Olympia
WASHINGTON
Salem
OREGON
Helena
MONTANA
NORTH DA
Bismarck
SOUTH DAK
Pierre
IDAHO
Boise
WYOMING
Cheyenne
NEBRASKA
Sacramento
Carson City
Salt Lake City
NEVADA
UTAH
Denver
COLORADO
CALIFORNIA
KANSA
ARIZONA
Santa Fe
Phoenix
NEW MEXICO
TEXAS
ALASKA
Juneau
Honolulu
HAWAII

MINNESOTA

St. Paul ★

WISCONSIN

Madison ★

MICHIGAN

Lansing ★

IOWA

Des Moines ★

Lincoln ★

ILLINOIS

Springfield ★

INDIANA

Indianapolis ★

OHIO

Columbus ★

PENNSYLVANIA

Harrisburg ★

VERMONT

Montpelier ★

MAINE

Augusta ★

NEW HAMPSHIRE

Concord ★

MASSACHUSETTS

Boston ★

Albany ★

NEW YORK

RHODE ISLAND

Providence ★

CONNECTICUT

Hartford ★

NEW JERSEY

Trenton ★

DELAWARE

Dover ★

MARYLAND

Annapolis ★

Washington, D.C. ☆

WEST VIRGINIA

Charleston ★

Richmond ★

VIRGINIA

Topeka ★

Jefferson City ★

MISSOURI

Frankfort ★

KENTUCKY

Nashville ★

TENNESSEE

Raleigh ★

NORTH CAROLINA

OKLAHOMA

Oklahoma City ★

Little Rock ★

ARKANSAS

ALABAMA

Atlanta ★

Columbia ★

SOUTH CAROLINA

Jackson ★

Montgomery ★

GEORGIA

LOUISIANA

MISSISSIPPI

Baton Rouge ★

Austin

Tallahassee ★

FLORIDA

N

W   E

S

The capital cities are marked with a star. Can you find the capital of the United States on this map?

Road Trip!

Malik lives in Ohio. His family is taking a trip to Georgia.

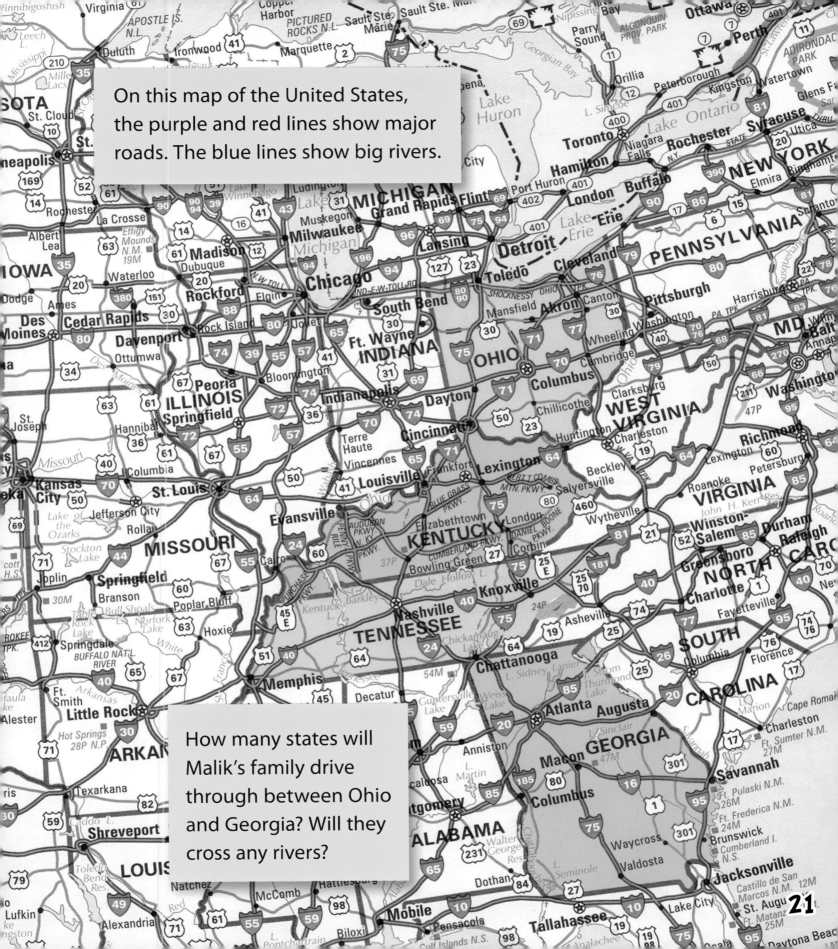

On this map of the United States, the purple and red lines show major roads. The blue lines show big rivers.

How many states will Malik's family drive through between Ohio and Georgia? Will they cross any rivers?

Globes

A globe is a special kind of map.

It is shaped like Earth. It shows the whole world.

Wow!

Look at all of the blue on the globe. Blue shows the water that covers Earth. There is more water than land.

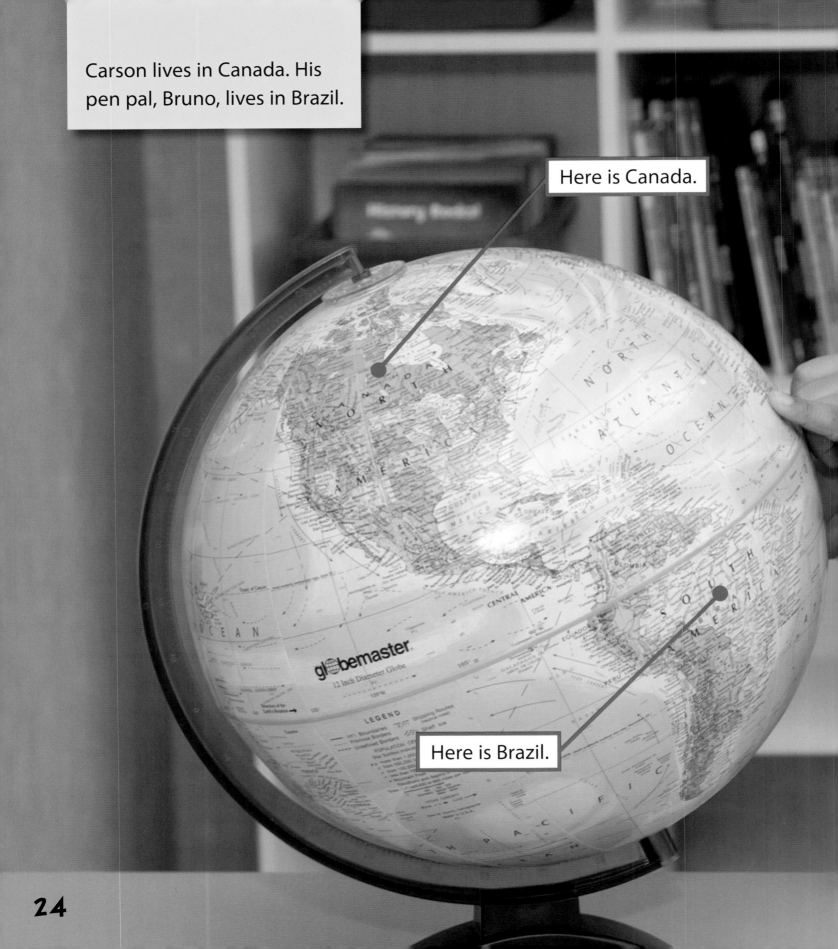

Carson lives in Canada. His pen pal, Bruno, lives in Brazil.

Here is Canada.

Here is Brazil.

24

Carson has to tilt the globe
to see where Bruno lives.

25

World Map

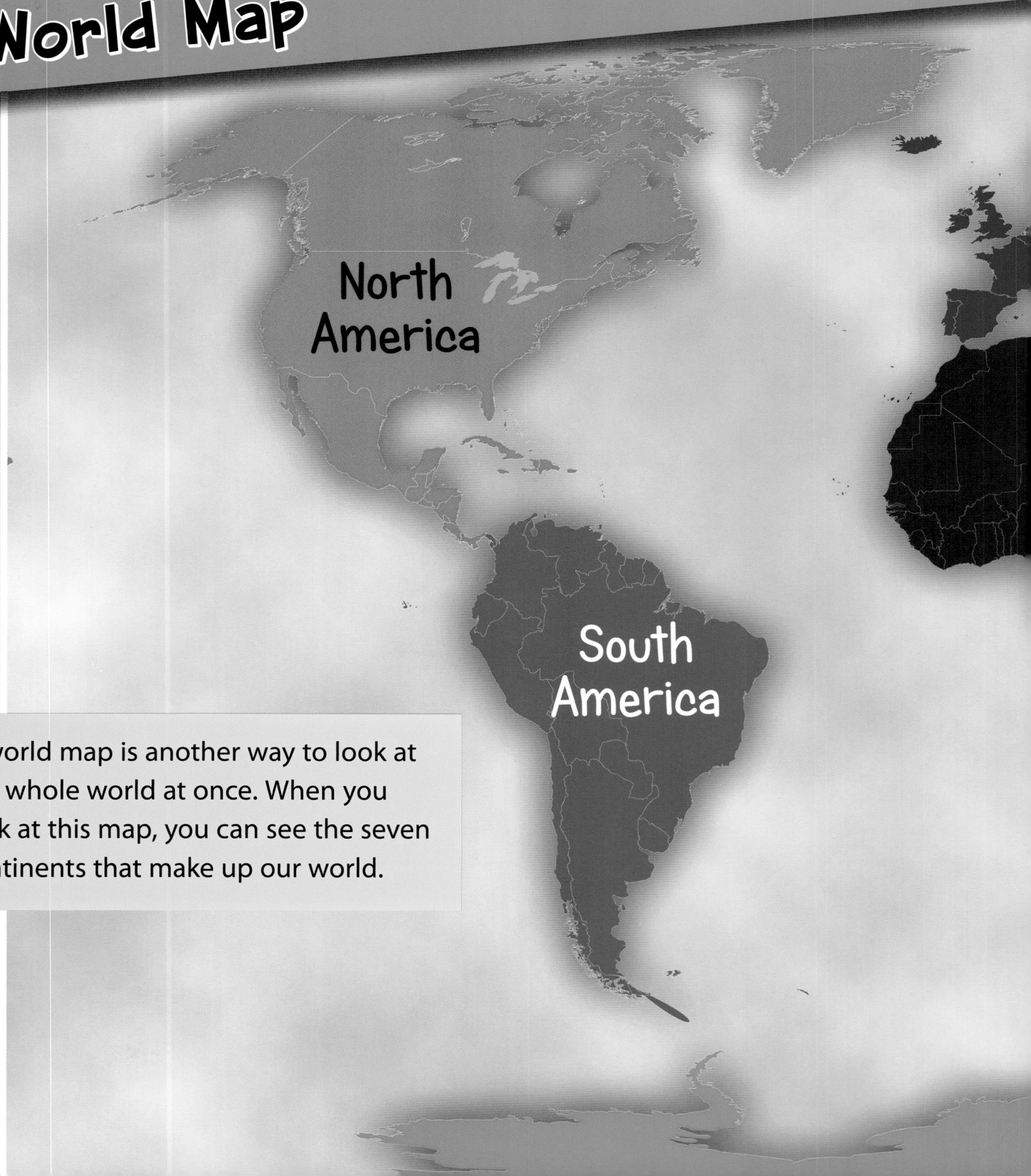

North
America

South
America

A world map is another way to look at
the whole world at once. When you
look at this map, you can see the seven
continents that make up our world.

Europe

Asia

Africa

Australia

Where is your continent?

Antarctica

27

Maps help us get around town and around the world. They tell us where to turn right or left, east or west.

What else can you use maps for? Finding treasure!

Where will a
map take you?

29

Glossary

boundary—a border that separates one area from another

capital—a city that is an official center of government

compass rose—a label that shows direction on a map

continent—one of Earth's seven large masses of land

key—a list or chart that explains symbols on a map or graph; a key is sometimes called a legend

route—the road or course followed to get somewhere

symbol—a design or an object that stands for something else

Critical Thinking Using the Common Core

1. Study the map on pages 18 and 19. Use the compass rose to tell which states are to the north and to the south of Kansas. (Key Ideas and Details)

2. Look at the map on page 11. Locate the gift shop on the map. Explain how you found the gift shop. (Craft and Structure)

3. Draw a map of your neighborhood. What parts of a map will you include on your map? Use the map on page 8 as an example. (Integration of Knowledge and Ideas)

Read More

Greve, Meg. *Maps Are Flat, Globes Are Round*. Little World Geography. Vero Beach, Fla.: Rourke Pub., 2010.

Jackson, Kay. *Ways to Find Your Way: Types of Maps*. Map Mania. Mankato, Minn.: Capstone Press, 2008.

Olien, Rebecca. *Map Keys*. Rookie Read-About Geography. New York: Children's Press, 2012.

Internet Sites

FactHound offers a safe, fun way to find Internet sites related to this book. All of the sites on FactHound have been researched by our staff.

Here's all you do:

Visit *www.facthound.com*

Type in this code: 9781476502625

Check out projects, games and lots more at
www.capstonekids.com

Index

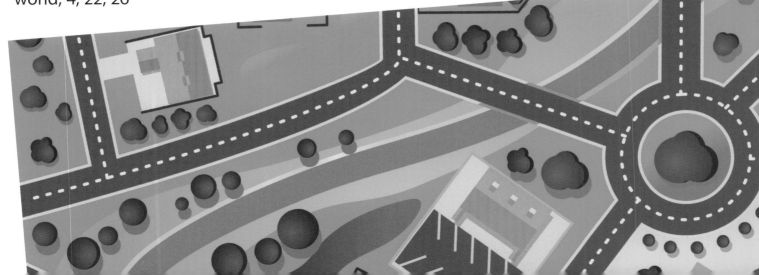